Praise for *Daddy Issues*

'This is a brave and brilliant book by one of the most insightful and articulate writers at work today. Katherine Angel is unafraid to look head on at the forgotten figure in feminism's critique of patriarchy: the father. All of us, daughters and sons, mothers and fathers, are enriched by confronting these libidinal energies, these daddy issues at the centre of all of our lives.'
— Lauren Elkin, author of *Flâneuse: Women Walk the City in Paris, New York, Tokyo, Venice, and London*

'A brilliant investigation into the father figure in culture that is also a powerful intervention in the #MeToo debate. Through it all, I think, sounds a call to be present for each other, attentive and open, willing to work for each other's full personhood.'
— Adam Foulds, author of *The Quickening Maze*

'In *Daddy Issues*, Katherine Angel holds the image of the father in a steady, critical gaze, generating both questions and hesitations, and opening up a vital space in which to challenge how power works in the family.'
— Dav⋯⋯ ⋯⋯ ⋯⋯ ⋯⋯ ⋯ *⋯ghts on*

'In this probing and erudite essay, Katherine Angel asks "Is it ever possible to get rid of the father, or is he forever internalised?" Angel traces the many ways that culture and life reflect the needs of father figures over and above those of "daughters", and how through both imagination and collective attention, we can begin to see and dismantle some of this power. A beautiful and necessary read.'
— Emilie Pine, author of *Notes to Self*

'In this impressive and intelligent examination of the father figure, Angel expertly intersects the subject with feminism, mythology, Donald Winnicott, Brett Kavanaugh and more. Her unstinting eye and intellectual vigour make *Daddy Issues* an engaging interrogation. It feels utterly vital in the context of #MeToo and the political flux the world currently finds itself in.'
— Sinéad Gleeson, author of *Constellations: Reflections from Life*

Copyright © Katherine Angel

The right of Katherine Angel to be identified as Author
of this Work has been asserted in accordance with
the UK Copyright, Designs and Patents Act 1988.

All rights reserved. No part of this book may be
reproduced or transmitted in any form without
the prior written consent of the publisher.

Every effort has been made to trace all copyright holders,
but if any have been inadvertently overlooked the publisher
will be pleased to include any necessary credits
in any subsequent reprint or edition.

A catalogue record for this book is
available from the British Library.

First published in 2019 by Peninsula Press

400 Kingsland Road
E8 4AA
London

peninsulapress.co.uk

Printed in Great Britain by CPI Group (UK) Ltd, Croydon

2 4 6 8 10 9 7 5 3 1

ISBN-13: 9781999922399

Daddy Issues

Katherine Angel

PENINSULA PRESS, LONDON
POCKET ESSAYS

For Matthew

'Nothing, my Lord.'
Cordelia, *King Lear*

In the awful, wearying months in which Harvey Weinstein's ritualistic mistreatment of women was being recounted daily in the media, I found myself, like so many others, wondering and talking about the men in my life: ex-boyfriends, ex-stalkers, ex-harassers, ex-gropers. My friends and I looked back, fitfully, in agitation, at the things we had endured, the things we had kept silent about, and we looked around at the things that were bothering us now. Throughout the autumn and winter, we told and re-told stories, seeing them in a new light, gently mentioning things we knew about one another's lives, murky memories, events we had not mentioned for years. We talked with a renewed anger and frankness, a renewed sense of permission in so doing—and perhaps, too, a renewed sense of simplicity. We were questioning all the men in our lives, all the forms of patriarchal power. But we rarely spoke about our fathers.

Soon after the allegations against him were published, Weinstein's wife Georgina Chapman announced she was leaving him. I kept thinking: what about his children? You can, at least in principle, leave a husband, but you can't leave a father.

In her poem 'Sunday Night', Sharon Olds describes her father, during family meals in restaurants, putting

> his hand up a waitress's
> skirt if he could—hand, wrist,
> forearm.

Olds notes that she never warned the young women.

> *Wooop!* he would go, as if we were
> having
> fun together.

She fantasises sticking a fork in his arm,
hearing 'the squeak of muscle', feeling 'the
skid on bone.'

> Sometimes
> I imagine my way back into the skirts
> of the women my father hurt, those
> bells of
> twilight, those sacred tented woods.
> I want to sweep, tidy, stack—
> whatever I can do, clean the stable
> of my father's mind.

Sharon Olds' project is reparative; she wants
to heal the wounds her father has inflicted—
she wants to use language to restore dignity
and pleasure. Can words rewind time, undo
harms? We might wish they could. But who
are we when we make this attempt? Who are
we writing as?

*

In her memoir *Fierce Attachments*, Vivian Gornick writes with horror of feeling consumed by her mother. She evokes familial intimacy as contamination, as infection:

> My skin crawled with her ... Her
> influence clung, membrane-like,
> to my nostrils, my eyelids, my
> open mouth. I drew her into me
> with every breath I took. I drowsed
> in her etherizing atmosphere.

Here, closeness is interpenetration of a dangerous kind; intimacy is drugging, threatening to consciousness, wakefulness, alertness. Boundaries are broken, or never established, and merging ensues. We inhabit, become, and reproduce our parents. They are in us; we are made of them, for good and for ill.

Sharon Olds, like Gornick, has written plentifully from her own life—about her parents, her husband, her children, her divorce—and has spent years navigating the agitated responses to such writing. It's generally assumed, and insisted upon, that writing from one's own life is the definition of exposure and of vulnerability. In some ways that is true, not least because the politics of speech and sexuality for women do make them vulnerable to judgement, to shaming, and to violence. But something else is sidelined by this insistence on the vulnerability of first-person writing, which is that writing isn't simply exposure: it is also protection. Writing is a spell; it conjures a person anew, and erects a protective wall. It can create a clear and ferocious distinction between self and other. It can enable the finding of a way 'to exist as oneself, and to relate to objects as oneself, and to have a self into which to retreat for relaxation.'

This is how psychoanalyst Donald Winnicott described the experience of 'feeling real'—an experience dependent on positive early parenting, on 'good-enough' mothering. (His language reflects the fact that it has usually been mothers who do the bulk of early parenting, though he underlined that the role of the good-enough mother can be fulfilled by others.) For Winnicott, this good-enough experience involved the mother's absorption in the infant; her flexible management of the infant's frustration and disappointment in her; and her ability to tolerate and survive the infant's aggression towards her. She must be able both to mirror the child back to itself, and to withstand its destructive impulses; be able to let him pursue a 'ruthless relation' to her, a 'benign exploitation' of her.

The formidable challenge of parenting is to nurture an environment which is, as Adam Phillips put it in his book on Winnicott, 'sufficiently resilient and responsive to withstand the full blast of the primitive love impulse'—and the full blast of aggression. 'Shall I say', wrote Winnicott, 'that, for a child to be brought up so that he can discover the deepest part of his nature, someone has to be defied, and even at times hated ... without there being a danger of a complete break in the relationship?'

*

Feminism and fathers have long been entangled, often in antagonism. Denouncing the patriarchal family has resonated for white, middle-class feminists in particular—women historically trapped in the bourgeois home, longing for emancipation from the family into the world of work. In 1938, Virginia Woolf's *Three Guineas* made powerful use of the figure of the father versus the figure of work. Her long essay is about the 'daughters of educated men' entering the professions, and it mulls on the effects of the 1919 Act that unbarred women from doing so: 'The door of the private house was thrown open'.

Woolf herself was no stranger to tyrannical, possessive fathers; her father Leslie Stephen formed the basis of her depiction of Victorian fathers in her fiction—in *The Years*, in *Night and Day*, in *To the Lighthouse*. Leslie Stephen enacted a suffocating domination of his daughters, particularly his stepdaughter Stella Duckworth, and all the more so after the death of their mother Julia Stephen.

Hermione Lee writes that, after Julia's untimely death, Leslie Stephen 'completely appropriated Stella as a substitute and she had allowed him to do it.' Woolf herself, in 'Reminiscences', written between 1907 and 1908, said that

> I do not think that Stella lost consciousness for a single moment during all those months of his immediate need... Sometimes at night she spent a long time alone in his study with him, hearing again and again the bitter story of his loneliness, his love and his remorse.

Stella was the audience for Leslie Stephen's grief, though she too was grieving; she was also expected to take on the work of looking after her half-sisters Virginia and Vanessa. Leslie, moreover, punished Stella for trying to leave the family home once she was to be married; her marriage was delayed by months due to his anguish. In 1939, in a piece entitled 'Memoir', looking back at this time as she periodically did, Woolf wrote:

> How the family system tortures and exacerbates... I feel that if father could have been induced to say 'I am jealous', not 'You are selfish', the whole family atmosphere would have been cleared and brightened.

No wonder Woolf held out hope for the world of work as the antidote to the stifling father. This was, in part, the argument of *A Room of One's Own*—it is money and independence from the family that enables women to write.

But it is the argument, too, of *Three Guineas*, in which she writes that if women are to wield influence, an influence apart from the vulnerable, dependent influence wielded within the patriarchal family, that influence will lie in being able to 'hold in their hands this new weapon, our only weapon, the weapon of independent opinion based upon independent income'.

This hierarchy of the public over the private—of the freedoms of professional life over the constraints of family—is entangled with social privilege, however. As bell hooks put it in 1984, 'Many black women were saying "we want to have more time to share with our family, we want to leave the world of alienated work".' And the workplace to which less privileged women have always been tied may not hold out the same alluring promise of freedom.

Yet Woolf has no illusions about either realm. The daughters of educated men are, she writes, 'between the devil and the deep sea. Behind us lies the patriarchal system; the private house, with its nullity ... its servility.' And then, tantalisingly but disappointingly, 'Before us lies the public world, the professional system, with its possessiveness, its jealousy, its pugnacity, its greed'—all words that could be applied to Leslie Stephen. Public and private alike are rotten for women.

Three Guineas charts the resistance of men to women's incursions into public life. Woolf was, while writing the essay, ruminating, with her familiar mixture of curiosity and ambivalence when assessing other writers' works, on the ideas of Freud that were garnering interest in England at this time. She describes fathers as 'massed together in societies, in professions', and reluctant to let their daughters out to work. 'Society it seems', she wrote, 'was a father, and afflicted with the infantile fixation too.'

Work, however, has not been the refuge it was hoped to be. In 'Revolutionary

Parenting', bell hooks writes, 'The women's liberationists who wanted to enter the work force did not see this world as a world of alienated work. They do now.' In recent years, public scrutiny of sexual harassment in the workplace has intensified, with good reason, though it has focused largely on the film and music industries, on the media and political classes—on Woolf's professions. Can this renewed scrutiny be usefully read as, among other things, a story of white, middle-class disillusion with the emancipatory promise of work?

*

Patriarchy—meaning the rule of men more generally, rather than simply the rule of fathers—was once a staple of feminist discourse, its cornerstone even. As an organising concept, however, it fell into some disrepute, due to the wishful universalism that characterised much of its invocation, the way that, in diagnosing such a simple problem, it seemed to hope for a simple solution. Just as the term 'woman' was queried, and feminists of colour in particular pointed out its frequent equation with white, middle-class womanhood, so too the other monoliths of feminism— such as patriarchy—were progressively destabilised.

Post-feminism further dented the ubiquity of patriarchy as a concept. The nineties— decade of girl power, and of an insistence on women's economic and social freedom, on the condition that women themselves abandon a critique of gender relations—gave invocations of patriarchy, as it gave feminism, a fusty feel, an old-fashioned whiff, conjuring all the age-old stereotypes of feminism: joylessness, sexlessness, uptightness.

Contemporary feminism has, however, re-embraced thinking about the big ideas— capitalism, work, care—and the concept of patriarchy is having a resurgence. In the waves of marches after Donald Trump's inauguration, it has featured heavily on banners; it circulates widely in highly instagrammable commodities, on t-shirts, on mugs, on tote bags. It is rolling around the mouths of pundits, commentators, and politicians. It's made a public comeback.

But for all the talk of patriarchy, has feminism forgotten about fathers? Fathers, and the heterosexual family more widely, are held in thrall. The relentless mawkishness of corporate advertising, whether for washing-up liquid or mortgages, features often childlike, cartoonish family figures dazedly embracing the requisite familial milestones: marriage, fond exasperation with muddy children, the family car, signing on the dotted line. And the cult of the family has extended beyond the heterosexual, not least because the right to a family life has been so cruelly forbidden to so many. The fight for equal marriage and equal parenting rights—the fight for equality in citizenship—has been, and still is, necessary and urgent. Yet, as Garth Greenwell has put it, fighting for these rights of citizenship comes with a risk—the risk that queer lives are translated into value that can be understood and approved of 'by people who hate queers'.

The push for equality, moreover, is utterly compatible with a vacuum of political thinking about the family; after all, it was David Cameron in the UK who made the push for equal marriage. In fact, the Tory party has long indulged in a bit of pinkwashing—a theatrical friendliness to kinship systems other than the heterosexual—in order to emphasise its political liberalism, all the while churning out punitive policies under the veil of 'austerity'. Cuts to legal aid for family work have left many women trapped in abusive marriages; the 'bedroom tax' has hit vulnerable individuals, such as those with disabilities, especially hard; and the two-child limit for tax credits, along with its cruel 'rape clause' requiring the disclosure of violence to qualify for exemptions, reveal just how routine it is for the veneration of family to go hand-in-hand with a blundering ignorance about the risks to individuals within the family itself. In 2018, Tory minister James Brokenshire denied that austerity policies have contributed to the shocking rise in homelessness since 2010, citing instead (among other causes) 'young people, because of their sexuality, being thrown out of home'—a strategic critique of homophobia used to defend the brutal social policies of a party with a historic, and enthusiastic, hostility to LGBT rights.

These days, sentimental dads get a lot of cultural cachet. New fathers, misty-eyed, proclaim their feminism when they first hold their newborn baby daughter. Overnight, they are transformed into heroic defenders of women's rights—though it's a defence that blurs into a defence of their daughters' purity; it relies, in other words, on an identification with a predatory masculinity that a father knows but now disavows; he sees into the dark soul of masculinity, now that he loves a creature he realises is vulnerable to its violence. And the adulation a father receives when he does the mundane, relentless work of parenting—when he 'helps' with the children, or 'babysits' them—reveals how ordinary acts of parental work and care add a glow of sanctity to a father, while passing unnoticed, because expected, in a mother. A 'hands-on' mother is a mother—the statement is a tautology—while a 'hands-on' father is a saint. We love a good Daddy.

*

Our contemporary concern about men—the men who perpetrate, enable, or turn a blind eye to violence against women—tends to hone in on men in our lives other than our fathers: our partners, friends, colleagues, bosses. Many, perhaps most, of these men are fathers too. Discontent with fathers has increasingly been privatised within feminist discourse; Daddy Issues have been relegated to the realm of personal problems. Yet fathers wield troubling power, whether they like it or not, and whether they claim or disown the patriarchal role history has given them. Valerie Solanas, in her *SCUM Manifesto* of 1967, wrote that 'the old-fashioned ranting, raving brute is preferable' to the 'modern, "civilized" father', as the brute is 'so ridiculous he can be easily despised'. Many men, perhaps aided by the saccharine cadences of advertising, and buoyed by the admiring compliments of strangers, are learning how to be better Daddies. But if we really want to think through the perpetuation of violence towards women, and towards all those deemed inferior in the hierarchy of masculine power, then we have to honour Solanas' thought. We need to keep the modern, civilised father on the hook.

*

Ginger and Rosa, Sally Potter's film of 2012, is set against the background of the Cuban missile crisis of 1962, and charts the agonies of seventeen-year-old best friends Ginger and Rosa. Ginger's mother Nat is a frustrated painter and now housewife to Roland, a pacifist and teacher who has previously been imprisoned for his activism. Rosa is raised by a single mother. The film is full of long panning shots of the windy, open landscapes the girls traverse, holding hands, their long hair blustering about their faces. They sit at bus stops; they stand at roadsides, hitching rides. Rosa sits in small rooms on springy single beds, writing poetry.

One night, Roland is driving the girls back to Rosa's house with the car roof down; he's speeding through tunnels, and they are exhilarated. As Rosa gets out of the car, she says, pointedly and not unflirtatiously, 'Bye, Ginger's Dad.' He replies: 'It's Roland, actually.'

Being a father is to be kindly, old, patriarchal, desexualised. Later, Ginger and Rosa hitch-hike, and are picked up by two older men, teddy-boys; speeding too, they drive the car onto a heath; the girls are being jolted all over the place. The car screeches to a halt, and the girls get out and run off.

Roland is a bad dad, but one of a leftist, radical stripe—he's no patriarch of the nineteenth-century, and no ranting, raving brute. He wants his daughter to be free and questioning and exploratory—but it's all a mirror-effect. He insists that Ginger calls him Roland, not 'dad', which, she explains to Rosa, ventriloquising her father, 'makes him think of slippers by the fire and other bourgeois death traps.' The girls, for their part, are choosing which patriarchal authority figure to revere. Rosa goes to church; Ginger goes to CND meetings in rooms packed with intoning men.

'Our mothers are pathetic', says Rosa one day; the absence of a man in her mother's life makes her scornful. 'They don't believe in anything', she goes on; 'or do anything, more to the point', agrees Ginger. 'Except moan about stuff.' Roland 'really hates the moaning', says Ginger. 'It's no wonder they can't keep their men', they agree.

Rosa and Roland begin sleeping together; she visits, cooks for him; she has become his housewife. Ginger's mother Nat is now living alone, returning to her painting. When Roland concedes that Ginger might not be happy with him sleeping with Rosa, Ginger says, 'How can anyone be happy when you know about the bomb? Happiness isn't an option when you know the whole world could be blown to pieces.' Roland replies, 'You're a good girl; a born radical, unsurprisingly.' While her bleak stance functions as a rationalisation of her depression and anguish, he sees in it a reflection of himself. He loves the sentiment because Ginger mirrors him, and, what's more, his praise expresses a relief that she has adjusted to low expectations of him. 'Daddy', wrote Solanas, 'wants what's best for Daddy.'

Girlhood is split, in the figures of Rosa and Ginger, between the girl who wants to sleep with the father, and the girl who wants to be the father. But there are other choices, ones Roland has made difficult for Ginger, by preventing her from pursuing a ruthless relation to him, by requiring her to perform a role for him. When the crisis comes—after Roland's self-indulgence is revealed to the adults—Rosa begs Ginger's forgiveness, begs for their friendship. In the final scene, Ginger faces us, her back turned to her father; she is writing a poem to Rosa, finally existing, perhaps, as herself in her act of creation. Roland, head in his hands, says 'I'm so sorry'. Ginger twists back to hear him, but says nothing, and turns back towards us, turns her attention back to her letter.

*

Sarah Moss's *Ghost Wall* is told from the perspective of a daughter, Sylvie—short for Sulevia, an Ancient British goddess. Sylvie, like Ginger, has been exquisitely, pathologically attuned to the parent's needs. Her father, Bill, is a bus driver who is obsessed with the Iron Age. He enlists his wife and daughter in joining a professor and his students on a summer expedition in rural Northumberland, part of a course in experimental archaeology. The aim is to live as ancient Britons might have. They forage, wear thin leather moccasins and scratchy tunics, and eat gruel; they sleep in a roundhouse on 'splintery bunks' padded with deerskins. While Sylvie shares one of these roundhouses with her parents, the three university students, Molly, Dan, and Pete, sleep in inauthentic, bright, waterproof tents in the clearing below. Sylvie offers to sleep there with the students and give her parents privacy, but her father refuses. 'Dad didn't want privacy, he wanted to be able to see what I was up to.' As Solanas put it, fatherhood is 'the male's major opportunity to control and manipulate.'

Sylvie's mother does the burden of the domestic work, trying gamely, though she has little choice, to prepare food as the ancients would have. Sylvie knows her mother is dominated; 'She had a new bruise on her arm.' Afraid of her husband, Sylvie's mother is anxious that Sylvie doesn't anger him, and enlists her in strategies of self-effacement. The two must go along with his plans, and the rituals they enact are rituals at the altar of a husband, a father. They must propitiate their own tyrannical god.

The Professor leading the experiment is more pragmatic, less fanatical than Sylvie's father; he wears tennis socks in his moccasins, for fear of blisters. The students, too, are less committed, aware of the silliness of dressing up in tunics, and they flaunt the rules, taking trips to the nearby Spar to get crisps, ice-cream, fizzy drinks. Molly refuses

to be intimidated by Bill, and her l[
fear enables Sylvie to fumble, ambiva[
towards a more honest yet infinitely more
painful perspective on her father.

She begins to voice, to herself at least,
the political motives pulsating under his
historical obsession, his desire for 'some
original Britishness'. But she prickles too;
she can sense that the students' scornful
mocking of her father's hobby—an important
source of identity and self-esteem—is a kind
of class snobbery. 'My dad, I thought, has as
much right to the Romans as you lot.' And
she senses the precarious masculinity that
is sustained and nourished by something
imagined to be grand, noble, powerful:

> The Wall was only a ditch, that first
> day, but at least it was a Roman ditch,
> a physical manifestation of Ancient
> British resistance still marked on the
> land, and you could see Dad drawing
> strength from it.

Sylvie sometimes ventriloquises her father, noticing herself parroting him to the students; she both identifies with, and is repulsed by him. She is torn between reproduction and rejection of him, and torn too between sharing her pain at his hands—his violence is gradually and horribly revealed by Moss—and defending the man whose love of the landscape she shares. It's hard to see your father criticised, even if he is a brute. Who knows what the daughters of the Weinsteins of the world feel about their dads?

Sylvie's father keeps at bay the possibilities of play, fun, and pleasure. Molly, in contrast, will not deprive herself. 'It's not as if Iron Age foragers wouldn't have gone to Spar if they could,' she says. It's a fair point. Why is Bill so attached to the idea of deprivation, of living without? He displays an attachment to the idea of work, even though what he is engaged in is a game, at least for him—a game whose work is done by his wife and

daughter, and whose nature as a game cann[.]
be admitted, for to do so would take away th[.]
heroic, hard-done-by ethos that gives him a
sense of purposeful masculinity.

In the summer heatwave, after a day of
foraging, Sylvie bathes naked in a shallow
stream, thinking she is out of sight. But her
father and the Professor appear. Bill hauls
Sylvie out of the water, 'eyes averted in
disgust.' 'You should be ashamed of yourself,
I'll not have my daughter a little whore', he
says. She dresses and he beats her with his
Iron Age leather belt.

> Stand against that tree, he said, a
> rowan not much taller than me...His
> arm rose and swung and rose again as
> the belt sang through the sunny air ...
> It went on longer than usual, as if the
> open air invigorated him, as if he liked
> the setting.

Molly confronts Sylvie about the marks

on her body. Sylvie may have useful skills while Molly doesn't—she knows where to find food, leading the students to bilberries on south-facing slopes—but Molly knows a patriarch when she sees one. And yet for Sylvie, violence and love are entwined:

> Maybe you're jealous because your dad left you, I thought, because he doesn't love you, because he doesn't care enough to teach you a lesson. Haven't you been listening, people don't bother to hurt what they don't love. To sacrifice it.

Sylvie, so identified with her father, seems to know where things are heading. A plan has been cooked up, secretively, by the men. One evening, the group discusses what they each would sacrifice to the bog that features so heavily in the book's physical and psychological landscape—the bog to which ancient people were sacrificed. The students and the Professor give their answers. Sylvie, who knows that 'you give what you most want to keep', feels 'Dad's eyes on me and knew with a shiver what he was thinking. My daughter. Break her and stake her to the bog, stop her before she gets away.' The men enlist Sylvie in their plan, and she grimly complies. Recounting this to an enraged Molly, she says:

> I'm sorry but I can't defy him, not
> over this, he's been thinking about this
> stuff for years, the bog people... I can't.
> Dad— your dad's not God, she said,
> he can't do anything he likes to you,
> however fascinated he might be.

Sylvie is resigned, and the terrible climax arrives. The Professor—modern, pacific, civilised—appears 'with a camera strung around his neck'. Bill 'laid a skein of rough rope around mine.' The Professor may not be the brute, but in the end it does not

ter; the two men are the same. 'You lead
er, Bill,' said the Professor, 'after all, she's
your sacrifice.'

Sylvie participates dissociatingly; stunned
into passivity, sadness leaking out of her.
Molly saves the day, with a local woman,
Trudi, whom she has befriended on her
trips outside the camp, though not before
Sylvie is injured. And after the violence, the
humiliation, the sheer cruelty, Sylvie is still
concerned for her father; her attachment is
still powerful. Trudi asks her about 'other'
harms, about touching; she is concerned
about sexual assault. 'No, I said, no, there
was nothing like that. He's my dad.' Despite
everything, she still trusts in the idea of the
father—*he's my dad*; she cannot acknowledge,
because it's too painful, that his being her
father hasn't prevented him from harming
her. Children protect what they have; Sylvie
rationalises the violence. Now safe with Trudi
and Molly, she is tended to by the women.
In the first moment of tenderness that we

see, of delicate and loving tou
sleeps protectively curled aroun
they are entwined. The book open
tenderness and solidarity between   ..en,
women weary with knowledge of the pains
men can inflict.

*

Fathers can of course inflict pain because of
their own suffering. Whereas Sylvie's father
is indulging his own fantasies of isolated,
self-sufficient masculinity, the father in
Leave No Trace, Debra Granik's 2018 film, is
pursued by traumatic memories. Unlike Bill,
this father is kind and gentle. A war veteran,
suffering from PTSD, he has created a world
in which he can cope; he and his thirteen-
year-old daughter Tom live in the forest, in a
makeshift but sturdy camp. Tom's father sells
on, to other homeless, tent-living veterans,
the drugs he has presumably been prescribed
for PTSD—this is how he makes money to

live on. This is a life, an environment, that is pretty resilient, but what does it disallow?

Always on the lookout for rangers, and adept at hiding and camouflaging their home, their work of survival is both a form of privation, and a form of pride; this father, too, has taught his daughter well. But his fear of interdependence and his mistrust of the social world have led to Tom being isolated, and sometimes also endangered. While his own trauma makes the confinement of urban spaces impossible, and while the lush, green, wet forests they live in have their own beauty and expansiveness, Tom cannot have friends; cannot have warmth; cannot have a social existence. Their life is always temporary.

Tom, like Sylvie, knows her father's feelings well, without necessarily knowing the details; infinitely attuned to his shifts of mood, she reassures him when he is anxious; when he wakes with nightmares, she talks with him, distracting him from the images and memories still haunting him. Later,

she finds a newspaper clipping amo...
documents her father keeps safely.
headline reads 'A Unit Stalked by Sui... ...,
Unable to Save Itself'.

Inevitably, their precarious existence is
interrupted; they are discovered by park
rangers and the police. A homeless service
takes them in, separately, and runs tests
on them. Tom defends her father against
questioners, against those who worry about a
father making his daughter live in a makeshift
home in the woods. The pair are re-housed,
in a bungalow, and a new life beckons. Tom
appreciates the comfort and interest her
new life affords her—some beginnings of
friendship, a bike, rabbits to pet. But it's all
too much for her father; he insists they leave.
They smuggle themselves onto freight trains,
and cross into Washington State, where the
higher altitude and greater cold make clear
the risks of this life to them both. Tom
suffers dangerously from the cold, and her
father is injured in the woods at night. Other

forest-dwellers help them, and one asks Tom, 'Where'd you live, where's your home?' Tom's reply is: 'My dad.' For Tom, home *is* the father, the father *is* home; the father is her landing-place. Like Sylvie in *Ghost Wall*, her radar sets to him; she tunes in to him, like a homing device.

Ultimately, Tom has to transcend the mothering role she's been asked to play, and she has to individuate; she has to extract herself from his troubled orbit. She, like Sylvie, understands the roots of her father's inability to father. She turns her back, in agony, in self-fulfilment, towards a life apart from him.

*

In an interview in 2007, when her father was not yet a presidential candidate but the host of *The Apprentice*, Ivanka Trump spoke about the ubiquity and enormity of his presence:

Increasingly, and especially with the

show, I've started to hear his voice
everywhere I go. I'll be driving and
I hear him come over the radio. I'll
be sitting on my couch typing on my
computer and I'll hear him on the
television, just this sort of voice of God
in the background. It's actually kind of
frightening as a daughter.

Ivanka has no privacy; she is welded onto
Donald, now the Daddy-in-Chief, the father
swollen to cosmic proportions. One of the
many disturbing things about the spectacle
of Trump in the White House is his
sexualised relationship to Ivanka. He assesses,
admires, and objectifies her as he might any
potential grabee.

Ivanka described Trump's notorious 'grab
them by the pussy' comments as 'clearly
inappropriate and offensive', but not without
adding that 'the greatest comfort I have is the
fact that I know my father.' She, like many
public daughters, serves as a validator for

her father. Trump, for his part, says, 'I've said that if Ivanka weren't my daughter, perhaps I'd be dating her.' He also says, 'You know who's one of the great beauties of the world, according to everybody? And I helped create her. Ivanka. My daughter, Ivanka. She's 6 ft tall, she's got the best body.'

*

Trump's creepy objectification of his daughter may in fact voice part of the cultural fabric that is no less disturbing for being disavowed. This thread goes deep in the culture: the assumption that there must be a kind of romance between father and daughter. The script of fathers and daughters has often looked like a contract, an agreement to mutually idolise. It has certainly been narrated this way culturally, from the virginity pledges associated with the Christian right in the US—the Silver Ring Thing—to the romantic comedies that take as their starting-point the rivalry between fathers and their daughters' boyfriends. It is the incestuous romance we are encouraged to fantasise.

And though we shudder at incest, we routinely reinforce the idea that a daughter in some way wants to sleep with her father. The very phrase 'daddy issues' both assumes and pushes away the idea that daughters desire their fathers. It is usually invoked to scorn or mock a woman's choice of sexual partner, whether due to his age, looks, status, or power; the suggestion is that she has fallen for a man who is a version of her father. The phrase admits this as a possibility, while denying and deriding it.

In *The Male Body*, philosopher Susan Bordo's exploration of masculinity told through a memoir of her father's life, Bordo writes that, aged eighteen, her father's sexual rage, jealousy, or protectiveness (what exactly does one call it?) left her 'confused about what I admired and wanted in a man.' Her father had pounded on her bedroom door after she had dared to close it on her and a boy, threatening to knock it down if they did not come out.

> It was embarrassing for a modern
> girl to have her father behave like a
> caveman. But these were the proofs
> of love my father offered, and they
> had an archetypal resonance that I
> couldn't deny.

A father's love is revealed in jealousy. But if there is a romance between father and daughter, however repressed, and however culturally determined, why are we so intent on it being the daughter's romance? We are alert to the daughter's daddy issues; what of the father's daughter issues?

*

In the 1991 remake of *The Father of The Bride*, a dishevelled Steve Martin, sitting among the

debris of a fairytale wedding—his daughter's—
speaks direct to camera. 'I'm told,' he says, 'that
one day I'll look back on all this with great
affection and nostalgia. I hope so. You fathers
will understand.' He then goes on to provide
us with the classic script of heterosexual
marriage, and of father–daughter relations:

> You have a little girl. An adorable
> little girl who looks up to you in a
> way you could never have imagined.
> I remember how her little hand used
> to fit inside mine. How she used to
> love to sit on my lap and lean her head
> against my chest. She said I was her
> hero.

The girl is non-sexual, though her adoration
of her father is intensely physical. She
is little, cute, and vulnerable; and her
devotion to her father is part of her
appeal, part of what moves him so much.

Then the day comes when she wants
to get her ears pierced. And wants
you to drop her off a block before the
movie theatre. Next thing you know
she's wearing eye shadow and high
heels.

We are supposed to know what this means;
we are meant immediately to understand
and identify with this father's horror
at his daughter's emerging sexuality,
and at his waning ability to control it.

From that moment on you're in a
constant state of panic. You worry
about her going out with the wrong
kind of guys. The kind of guys who
only want one thing. And you know
exactly what that one thing is, because
it's the same thing you wanted when
you were their age.

This father has gained distance from his earlier

virile self, though he also identifies with it—
and identifies with the younger man he is
being displaced by. The daughter becomes the
girl that he, once upon a time, was chasing.

> Then she gets a little older, and you
> quit worrying about her meeting the
> wrong guy, and you worry about her
> meeting the right guy.

We're supposed to feel impossibly moved
by this moment, I think—moved by
the realisation that a father's irrational,
possessive, aggressive behaviour, the
behaviour we intuit we're going to see
unfold, can in fact be explained by love.
It was all about love! *Le crime passionnel.*

> That's the biggest fear of all because
> then you lose her. And before you
> know it, you're sitting all alone in a big
> empty house, wearing rice on your tux,
> wondering what happened to your life.

His own wife has been written out of this fairytale; she has become invisible, and the locus of sexual charge is the daughter, who figures as the perennially young woman a man is always chasing in his heart. The daughter's own desires, her feelings and agency, are, of course, also obscured and displaced here. Her relationship is, after all, really all about her father. The daughter figures as a symbol of the father's sexuality too; his life is co-eval with his daughter's innocence. Once that is gone, his life is over. Can a father not survive a girl's entry into the sexual realm? As long as she is still oriented towards him, and as long as he is undisplaced by a lover, his sexual potency is still in play. Once she has turned away from him to another man, it is his sexual power that is placed in question.

After this speech, we go back in time to the daughter's surprise engagement, and the ensuing action is jam-packed with the familiar tropes. The father is appalled by the news of the engagement: horrified, angry, jealous, unable to conceal his wounded sense of having been displaced. He acts comically badly towards the fiancé; when his daughter and the new man kiss, he rolls his eyes, while the mother whimpers in admiration. The father identifies as a jilted lover, while the mother identifies with a romantic girlhood. The audience is presumably meant to do the same, in line with their gender. Later in the film, Martin bitterly acknowledges that 'my day has passed', likening himself to 'an old shoe, discontinued.'

But is the father's horror at his daughter's sexuality exactly that? Or is it a displaced horror at his own sexuality, his own desire? The commonness of sexual abuse of teens, and the ubiquity of the teen trope in pornography, would suggest that most men at least know what it's like to desire a teenage girl. Is the father's horror at his daughter's sexuality perhaps a disavowed horror at his own susceptibility to it?

*

Since the de-contractualising of marriage, the question of ownership of the daughter has taken on a romantic and sexual hue. Marriage is no longer an exchange of property, but the exchange of a desired love object. While it is still understood, consciously or unconsciously, as about ownership, the question of ownership is now overwhelmingly cast in the rosy light of love.

In Hollywood, a father's sexual jealousy is always taken for granted. In *Meet the Parents*, Greg meets his new girlfriend Pam's parents for the first time on the occasion of Pam's sister's wedding. They stay at Pam's parents' house. Robert De Niro plays Pam's father Jack, supposedly a retired florist who is really an ex-CIA operative. The set-up is classic: an alpha male father, competitive with—and hostile to—the new boyfriend, convinced no one is good enough for his daughter.

The entire family defers to monomaniacal

father Jack, taking this rivalrous dy
as given. When Pam and Greg arri
the house, and Pam detects her fat..₋₁s
immediate animosity, she says to him, with
fond affection, 'Be nice to this one, Dad, I like
him.' The normalisation of the father's sexual
jealousy, and his hostility to his replacement,
are firmly established; we know in advance
that things will go horribly wrong, and are
being primed to both dread and long for the
dénouement, with this casual, parenthetical
admission that *this is what fathers do*. None of
this disturbs us. Why?

*

A father, historically, protects a daughter—
and to the extent that he protects her, it's
her value that he is protecting, as a piece
of property to transfer. He is therefore the
guardian of her virginity, her modesty,
her shame. A father reluctantly lets her go
into the world of men; suitors must travel

via him, assuaging his worries about their intentions. The complicit resignation, the professed horror of the father at the potential caddishness of the suitor, have always struck me as shaded with pride, with a pleasure taken in identification and recognition. A father warns his daughter about men's intentions, their shallowness and crudeness; a father thereby warns his daughter about himself, his past self, too. I am a man, I know what it is to be a man; I was like them, and now I must warn you about them. I am warning you about myself; be careful. The father is not, in fact, instructing the daughter in the woeful ways of men, but is addressing the audience in his pride about them.

*

And yet none of this can be named. *The Archers*, Radio 4's epic, long-running soap about a fictional farming village, also mines this dynamic: not the oedipal desire of the daughter for the father, but the fraught, disavowed desire of the father for the daughter, via his identification with other men. David Archer, a farmer in his late fifties, has long displayed an over-investment in the romantic and sexual life of his daughter Pip. For years I wondered if the strangeness of the scenes, the uncomfortable tension between them, was an acting problem; it was as if David and Pip were ex-lovers, talking awkwardly, trying to manage their over-entanglement in one another's lives while pretending to be cool. And David and his wife Ruth often speaks with Pip about her love-life, in a way that seems to me unconvincing; would a teenage girl not want more privacy from her father? Would she not resent the mere fact of his intrusions, not simply the content of them? (He often disapproved of her men.) Perhaps this was just bad writing. I came to believe, however, that the scriptwriters knew exactly what they were doing, and were playing a long game; that, for all the cheery villagey Englishness of it, the series is in fact an astute exploration of the profoundly different experiences of men and women in the heterosexual family.

David hated teenage Pip's boyfriend Jude Simpson, the motorbike-riding, older student bad boy. He hated her boyfriend Toby Fairbrother, the posh, hapless cad. And he has been troublingly close to Pip; in one painful phase for the family, when David's wife Ruth was often away caring for her ill mother, the sense of David and Pip becoming the marital couple became overwhelming and hard to ignore. Ruth felt it, and was hurt and jealous.

What's more, David feels outraged when it becomes repeatedly clear that his daughter chooses sexual partners who are not remotely like him. He takes his daughter's sexual life personally, and fails to consider that his over-investment, his entitlement to airing his feelings about her sexual choices, is inappropriate. When Pip became pregnant, David was outraged that his sister

Elizabeth knew about it before he and Ruth did. Others—Ruth, for example—sometimes take him to task for his being harsh with Pip's boyfriends; yet no one challenges his narcissistic relation to the boyfriends, his effective insertion of himself as Pip's rejected lover, his insinuation of himself as the figurehead of masculinity whom Pip must either mirror or reject in her choices.

And yet perhaps David is simply voicing what is a long-standing, and naturalised, if not necessarily natural, aspect of fatherhood. Leslie Stephen, Virginia Woolf's father, wrote in 1896 in a letter to Charles Norton, 'I am ... practicing for the new position of father-in-law'—his stepdaughter Stella was about to marry. He went on:

> To tell you a profound secret, I find
> that it has its difficulties... I could
> do perfectly well without Jack—
> Why should not she? Is my feeling
> something abnormal and discreditable

> to a father, or is it natural—a result,
> perhaps, of the jealousy wh. makes the
> man look askance at the devotion of
> any woman to anybody but himself?

His identification with his step-daughter is nearly total; he is unable to distinguish between self and other. At least Leslie Stephen, in this letter, was aware of his own jealousy, understanding it to be all about himself—though Woolf lamented his inability to say to Stella, or indeed to her, 'I am jealous', rather than 'you are selfish'. Her father's feelings dominated domestic life, and Woolf famously wrote that had he lived, 'his life would have entirely ended mine.' If fathers could acknowledge their jealousy, and their projection—their annexing of their daughters' erotic life to their own vanity, their annexing of their daughters' subjectivity to their own—these daughters might suffer less, and we might all give up assuming women's choices must revolve around a man's jealousy.

Possessiveness and over-identification,

incidentally, have their inevitably cruel lining. In the painful saga of Meghan Markle's now all-too-public difficulties with her erratic father Thomas, he has retaliated for what he sees as her pushing him out of her life. 'What riles me,' he told the *Daily Mail*, 'is Meghan's sense of superiority. She'd be nothing without me. I made her the Duchess she is today. Everything that Meghan is, I made her.' In rhetoric reminiscent of Trump's prideful appropriation of Ivanka's body— his narcissistic claim to ownership of her physical attributes—Thomas Markle does something similar; a daughter's identity, and a daughter's achievements, belong to her father. And when a father finds himself displaced, he can turn punitive, expelling from himself what he has hitherto seen as his own mirror.

*

In Sophie Mackintosh's *The Water Cure*, three sisters, Lia, Grace, and Sky, live in a grand house bordered by water, with their pinched mother and revered father, known as King. Beyond their anxiously surveyed home, on the other side of a dangerous sea, is a world against whose infection and horrors the girls must be guarded. Mother and King orchestrate the girls in a series of protective rituals, designed to keep them healthy against the encroaching poisons of the world outside. There are breathing rituals; falling rituals; painful exercises in which Mother aims hard balls into the girls' ankles; games of commanded cruelty: the daughters must drown a mouse, or burn a frog—though, at the last minute, when the frog has been thrown into the fire, Mother throws water over it and the frog hops out. For the girls, these are tests of love, obedience, and devotion; they are being asked, as the Biblical Abraham and Issac were, to do and bear the unbearable. King is both Lear and Prospero in one; Prospero, orchestrating life and action on his apparent island, conducting the daughters

in scream therapy with a conducting baton;
Lear, exacting devotion from his daughters,
putting them in a bind of demanded love.

The girls are trained in postures of
abasement and gratitude (Lia gratefully
takes 'whatever contact I can get'), postures
which have as their rationale the fortifying
of the self against the cruelties of the world.
As I read *The Water Cure*, an ironising phrase
from Woolf's *A Room of One's Own* rang in my
ears; it occurs when she describes being, as a
mere woman, shooed officiously off the lawn
in an Oxbridge college: 'the gravel is the place
for me.'

King, warning the girls of the men beyond
the border,

> spoke of perverse appetites. He spoke
> of bodies grown strong despite the
> toxic air ... Men like that would break
> your arm without thinking. 'Like this',
> he had said, demonstrating on us,

clasping both fists around each of our forearms in turn and making as if to snap. We felt the bone threaten to give, stayed calm. 'And worse.'

The novel probes the violence inflicted on women in the name of their protection. But it probes something else too: fathers as a route into reality. For a long time, we are not sure if the fantasies of infection, of exposure and vulnerability in which the girls are trained, are true or not. Is this a fiction designed to keep the daughters close? The novel, in pressing this question, uncovers the dysfunctional power at the heart of the patriarchal family, the cult-like devotion that family can engender. And what happens when the father lies?

Freud's Oedipus complex sees selfhood as constituted through certain painful crises. The boy's fantasy of sexual union with the mother is broken from the outside by the father, and his fantasy of killing the father comes up against his inability to compete with the father's phallic power. Under the imagined threat of castration, the boy renounces his erotic investment in the mother. For the girl, the discovery of the absence of the penis creates the fantasy of having been castrated; this creates a turning away in horror from the mother, imagined similarly to have suffered this fate. The girl's desire for a penis is transferred to the desire to bear her father a child.

In the Oedipus complex, it is the father's intervention in the child–mother dyad that enables individuation. The father is the traumatic but all-powerful vehicle through which a child turns away from the mother, and ultimately towards heterosexual relations. The complex's repressions and sublimations of desire, moreover, are the means through which social and cultural life are made possible.

There is much to contest about the Oedipus complex, not least its heteronormative constraints. Nonetheless, it is a powerful rendering of the father as both source of refusal and source of possibility. The father is a figure of disillusion—he drives a brutal, awakening wedge into the blissful, imaginary union of the child and mother. He is therefore a figure of constraint. Lacan built on this image of the father; the 'nom-du-père' (which translates as the *name* of the father while punning on the *no* of the father) is the cornerstone of his revision of the Oedipus complex. The father prohibits. 'Every boy', wrote Solanas, 'wants to imitate his mother, be her, fuse with her, but Daddy forbids this.'

And yet the father is also the enabler of the future, of maturity, of social life. Lacan dwelt not just on sexual prohibition, but on the father's intrusion into the child–mother dyad in a symbolic capacity, and the child's entry into language. Within the history of psychoanalysis, the father has been, in Jessica Benjamin's words, the 'father of liberation' versus the 'mother of dependency'.

In *The Water Cure*, the father disappears—
but his reach is long, and the novel charts the
far-reaching effects of his patriarchal power.
King never entirely disappears; his absence is
never fully realised, in part because Mother
does his work so well, and in part because
patriarchy, like all power, is productive as
well as repressive. King is the girls' route
into reality, but they find that this reality
is a fiction. The toxicity they fear does not
in fact exist in the form they were taught; it
lies instead not just in the bodies of the men
they were warned against, but in the family
forms that ostensibly schooled them in it.
As in *Ghost Wall* and *Leave No Trace*, these
girls move beyond attachment to the father,
and beyond attachment to any man; they
move beyond the Oedipus complex towards
identification with one another, with their
sisters, and towards the possibilities of rage,
violence, and resistance. The final chapter
culminates in narration in the voice of all
three daughters. 'There is something rising

in us,' they say, 'and I am glad'. There are intimations of violence here, faint tremors of Solanas' Manifesto: 'If SCUM ever strikes, it will be in the dark with a six-inch blade.' It will 'coolly, furtively, stalk its prey and quietly move in for the kill.'

*

In *Leaving Neverland*, Wade Robson and James Safechuck, the two men giving accounts of their sexual abuse by Michael Jackson, spoke frankly of their desire, at the time, to be with him. They spoke of the pleasure they sometimes took in the sex; of having felt painfully, deeply in love with him, felt agonisingly jealous of Jackson's new young favourites, and protective of him in the face of allegations (both had previously testified in Jackson's defence). The boys wanted to sleep over at Neverland, and the abuse occupied a painful, unprocessed, darkened place in their psyches and bodies.

Wade Robson, an Australian dance prodigy obsessed with Jackson from a very young age, became friends with Jackson—and danced on stage with him—when he was five years old. The abuse started when Robson was seven, on a visit to the US. Not long after, Robson's mother moved her son and daughter to the US, largely in order to pursue dance dreams promised by Jackson, and to be near him. The father and older brother stayed behind; the family never fully reunited, and the father later died by suicide.

The men spoke of their fear of outing Jackson, who had repeatedly told them that he and they would go to jail if found out. But another fear may also have been crucial; the fear of puncturing the collective fantasy about Jackson, the collective investment and enchantment in him. *Leaving Neverland* revealed the extent to which Jackson's enchantment of a young boy was simultaneously the enchantment of a whole family; the magical unbelievability of this global star showing up at the house, seeking refuge there, and behaving like a sweet child himself, was evidently too much to resist or question. The mothers in the documentary spoke of feeling maternal towards Jackson, of how childlike he was; mother and son alike fell in love with the man-child that Jackson was. He was like a brother to the boys, went the refrain, and like a son to the mothers; but in certain undeniable ways he was also like a father and a husband: all-powerful, irresistible, the sun around whom the family orbited; the figure one could not destroy.

Both men said they still loved Jackson. The term 'seduction', when abuse is discussed, sounds at best old-fashioned, and at worst inappropriate, equating as it seems to do abuse and romance: let us name abuse as abuse! But in fact that the word is disturbingly apt: abuse is partly about seducing someone, making them feel special and loved. It brings them into orbit, casts a spell on them—so that there is something they gain from staying close, something they gain from not outing the abuser. It's about clouding judgement, creating investments, including the selective blindness of love, and fearing an imagined separation, a separation that will nullify one's existence. The powerful cement of the loving gaze can make a child tolerate, or keep silent about, manifest abuses of power. It was impossible for these boys, given everyone's enchantment by Jackson, given his seduction of almost the entire family, to countenance pulling the rug out from under the shared fantasy. How do you bring an entire edifice down? The boys' fathers were replaced by Jackson; a man whose childlike surface concealed a patriarchal force. There can only be one Daddy, and Jackson had taken up residence.

*

Is it ever possible to get rid of the father, or is he forever internalised? When we repudiate the father, or when he disappears, are we free of our Daddy Issues? The politics of speech and truth-telling tempt us to believe that naming the truth about various patriarchs—Woolf's fathers 'massed together in societies and professions'—is the key to our freedom. But it's not clear that this is the case.

In 2018, against the background of Brett Kavanaugh's confirmation to the US Supreme Court despite credible allegations of sexual assault by Christine Blasey Ford, Jia Tolentino wrote in the *New Yorker* that 'women's speech is sometimes wielded, in this #MeToo era, as if it were Excalibur—as if the shining, terrible truth about the lives of women will, by itself, vanquish the men who have exploited and controlled them.' She describes the attachment to this idea as 'a sort of delusive optimism'. And she notes that truth-telling does not automatically throw open the doors of justice, raze the ground, redress inequity—and that it may, perversely, entrench misogyny. 'It will be said', she writes, 'that Kavanaugh was confirmed despite the #MeToo movement. It would be at least as accurate to say that he was confirmed *because* of it.' Solanas' ranting, raving brute, and her modern, 'civilized' father alike may take pleasure in hearing of women's pains at the hands of brutes. The evidence of swaggering cruelty may both gratify and solidify the fantasy of dominance. Me too, many men must have felt on watching the hearings—I too could be Kavanaugh, acting with impunity, enacting my *droit de seigneur* in the highest court of the land.

Not long after the allegations against Weinstein emerged, comedian John Oliver questioned Dustin Hoffman, at a public event, about historic sexual harassment allegations made against the actor. Hoffman was, predictably, flustered, defensive, and angry. It's not clear to me that Oliver was wrong to do this, but it's not clear to me that he was right, either. The spectacle made me uncomfortable; why? In one sense, it was the longed-for sight: of men being made accountable, of injustices being brought to light, of a refusal to defer to powerful social norms. A gratifying spectacle, then; should I not have been pleased? Perhaps my discomfort had to do with fear. Sylvie, in *Ghost Wall*, has intimate knowledge of this particular fear; 'you don't make him feel stupid'. It is when men feel humiliated that they are most capable of violence.

But my discomfort may have stemmed from something else too. Oliver got to feel really good, I suspect, about this moment. It is easier for someone who is not implicated in this particular dynamic to call someone out for their behaviour. What made me uncomfortable was that this spectacle—this welcome spectacle, even—of a man holding another man to account, was subject to the same logic of punishment and humiliation as the cruelty it was ostensibly challenging. At the heart of this exchange was a display of power asserted over another, and a pleasure taken in the other's abject position. There is undeniably a pleasure to be taken in humiliating the agent of your own humiliation; it's gratifying to see the bad Daddy fall. But I'm not sure I believe in humiliation as a tool for progress.

The anger and rage we might feel towards a father, towards the patriarch—towards the raving brutes or the civilised fathers—is not something we can expel, once and for all, and nor does it yield a clear solution. Rage has instead to be folded into everything else we may simultaneously feel; it does not simply burn itself out. What's more, love and hate are not opposites, but are developmentally entangled. We have to be able to hate in order to love.

*

There are people whom I cannot look in the eye in conversation. Avoiding eye-contact is often seen as a sign of guilt or shame, but it can also be an attempt to resist being used. The people whose eyes I cannot meet are those in whose gaze I can detect the overwhelming clamour of requested affirmation; those in whose gaze lies a demand for recognition, and a request for compliance. I hate to be made into the mother whose maternal gaze is demanded, the gaze of mirroring and recognition. When I only exist as a mirror for someone else, I cannot go on looking.

In 2018, Anthea Hamilton's *Squash* took up residence at Tate Britain, in the imposing Duveen galleries now dotted with various podiums and a swimming-pool-like stage. Everything was porcelain-like, gleaming and clean—clinical in its brightness. The day I went, the Squash—performed, or embodied, by a rota of actors—was sitting on a square, armchair-like structure. I approached from behind, could see the round bulb of its head, and its relaxed, confident pose. Moving round it, I saw the Squash more clearly: a human figure, dressed that day in floaty clothes, a full dress with a velvet-looking panel at the chest and somewhat puffed sleeves. It was wearing bright yellow and green gloves, thick and sturdy like those used for gardening. A beautiful, bulbous, obscene squash-like structure covered its entire head, the colours salmon pink and emerald green, marbled like Florentine endpapers. Its sort-of-nose was long—animal, vegetable, and genital all at once.

It sat, imperious though not unfriendly, looking out at a bemused audience. People strolled by and stopped in curiosity; some rushed past, disconcerted; one woman visibly shuddered and, catching my eye, pulled a face—the Squash was uncanny, for sure. Others failed to notice it at all. For its part, it sat watching us, calmly, placidly, a human-animal-vegetable, deliciously genderless, a formidable projective screen. I watched it for ages, hypnotised by its ambiguous, connotative form, its lack of face as such, its absence of discernible needs or investments in anyone else's gaze. At one point I sensed its awareness of my prolonged staring, but seeing no eyes, no face, I felt able to stay there and keep looking. When I eventually moved round to the back of it to leave, its great, lovely head turned heavily with my movement, slowly following me.

It was such a relief to look at the Squash; to hold and be held by a gaze I could not really see; to experience an exchange of gazes free of anxiety, desire, investment, demand. How wonderful it would be to not have to see people's faces, with all their needs and longings and projections! And to have one's face unseen, one's own face with all its needs and longings and projections.

*

In *The Kiss*, published in 1997, Kathryn Harrison tells the story of her incestuous relationship with her father—a father who leaves her and her mother when Harrison is an infant, and whom she only sees a couple of times before her late teens. It's in these late teenage years that they are reunited, and the relationship begins. Nominally consensual, the sex is something Harrison is reluctant to have with her father, though she is frank about her deep yearning for him, her obsessive attachment. Her life quickly unravels; he comes to dominate and constrain her life, and her shame and confusion isolate her deeply. Her father, tellingly, is hard to classify in Solanas' neat taxonomy of civilised versus brute; he is a terrible mixture of both.

In a vicious review of the book, James Wolcott asked: 'remember when it took some digging to unearth secrets?' Now, he says, 'the problem is the opposite: getting people to put a cork in it.' Bemoaning what he sees as a rash of memoirs and autobiographical novels, he calls *The Kiss* 'trash with a capital "T"'. Wolcott turns down no opportunity to slut-shame, befuddled by the possibility that something nominally consensual can nonetheless not be freely chosen, or can also be exploitative. He describes the book as narcissistic, on the grounds that Harrison 'craves the public spotlight as deeply as she did her father's heat-seeking eyes.'

It's wrong, however, to describe *The Kiss* as a narcissistic book. On the contrary, it's a book that is profoundly, and self-knowingly, about narcissism. It is rife with fairytale symbolism—a kiss that sends Harrison to sleep, a kiss that awakens; a cut-off ponytail offered as a sacrifice. Harrison tells her story with a startling lucidity, a spare and stark control; *The Kiss'* measured, balletic cadences are narrated with a calm analytic precision that is unsettling. And it plays overtly with the mirrors and reflections of the Narcissus myth, exploring precisely those symbolic elements that shape our family relationships.

Harrison's parents separated soon after she was born. When Harrison is still a young child, her mother moves into her own flat, leaving Harrison in the care of her grandparents. Her mother visits, she is still involved, but at a remove, and she is depressed, remote. Harrison dwells frequently on the gaze; on sight, looking, and mirrors. Her father is a missionary, and after reading his postcards from abroad, describing poor and underprivileged children with crossed eyes, Harrison, 'ashamed that I don't persevere bravely in a slum, and ashamed of my clear vision', begins to cross her eyes experimentally.

'My mother sleeps', Harrison tells us. 'For as long as she lives with us, in her parents' house, she sleeps whenever she can.' She describes standing beside her mother's bed, fantasising the power to wake her up. She knows that 'for as long as my mother refuses consciousness, she refuses consciousness of me: I do not exist.' She watches her mother's face concealed by a satin sleep mask; sleep 'makes my mother's face itself into a mask, one mask under another'. Sometimes

Harrison lifts the mask. 'Her eyes, when they turn at last toward me, are like two empty mirrors. I can't find myself in them.'

It is through the mirror of the other's eyes that we learn to experience ourselves as existing in infancy. For Lacan, the encounter with the mirror enables the infant to make an imaginary identification with its reflected image. The mirror provides the infant with a gratifyingly coherent image of itself as unified, an image that provides relief from an experience of fragmentation by granting an illusory sense of bodily unity. But the mirror is not faithful; it distorts and deforms; the child is still dependent on others for physical security; it is not whole and autonomous in the way the mirror suggests, but rather a cacophony and multiplicity of drives and desires. The self therefore recognises itself through misrecognition; the self-unity the mirror enables the infant to 'recognise' is a fiction.

The subject, therefore, develops an image

of itself by identifying with an image brought in from the outside. And yet, as Winnicott writes, 'the precursor of the mirror is the mother's face'. The tendency in psychoanalysis to see mother–infant merging as both illusory and preparatory, as that which occurs *before* reality sets in— the father of liberation versus the mother of dependency—was challenged by numerous revisions to the Oedipus complex and a shift of focus to pre-Oedipal interactions. The deeply active and developmentally significant care of mother–infant interactions was underlined in the return of postwar British psychoanalysis—by Winnicott and Melanie Klein in particular—to the mother (Freud had not been much interested in the mother's minute but momentous work in child-rearing).

For Winnicott, the role of the mother is 'of giving back to the baby the baby's own self'. When the infant looks at his mother's face he can see himself, and how he feels, reflected back in her expression. He can only discover what he feels by seeing it mirrored back. If the infant is seen in a way that makes him feel he exists, in a way that confirms him, he is free to go on looking. If his mother is preoccupied by something else, when he looks at her he will only see how *she* feels. He will not be able to get 'something of himself back from the environment'.

The mother, however, must not be purely a mirror; she must not merely reflect the child back to itself, but must, says Jessica Benjamin, 'embody something of the not-me'. The child, she writes, 'enjoys a dose of otherness.' The constant back and forth between recognition and resistance is what helps the infant discover, with the mother, not just her, but reality. Yet many things can inhibit this capacity in a mother: depression, fear, anxiety, and the frustration of her own longings and ambitions. No wonder mothering can be such hard, exhausting work. As a character in Jenny Offill's *Dept. of Speculation* puts it to the mother protagonist, 'you are creating a creature with a soul'.

The encounter with the mirroring parent who doles out doses of otherness, bringing into being the child's sense of itself, is what Harrison seems to have lacked as a child, from either parent. The need and the longing to be seen—to be made real by the parent—is overpowering. Children need the interactive, me-not-me gaze of those who love them in order to experience themselves as subjects with agency; they need a gaze which is itself uncontaminated by a parent's need to see themselves reflected back by the child, a gaze untrammelled by the parent's desire to find themselves, and their perhaps own longed-for maternal gaze, in the child.

When Harrison is eighteen and reunited with her father, his gaze—so longed for—is both gratifying and intrusive. "'Don't move", he says. "Just let me look at you."' His 'besotted focus is intoxicating'. He looks at her 'as no one has ever looked at me before.'

Whatever Harrison does—'peel an orange, tie my shoe, pour water from a pitcher into the dry soil of a house-plant'—enthrals him.

> I get up to brush my teeth, and he
> follows me into the bathroom. He
> leans against the doorjamb to watch
> as I squeeze the paste from the tube.
> His scrutiny both excites and exhausts
> me.

Photographs, too, are key. Her father, a keen photographer, understands the power of the mirror image, intuits that we come to have a sense of self through a reflected image. He 'stands back and puts the camera before his eyes. "I'll have to show you who you are", he says. "I'll have to do it with this." The shutter clicks, and clicks.'

Harrison goes from being un-seen—by both mother and father—to being over-seen by her father. Her father is 'the lost father', whom she is always seeking to retrieve—but this search is an attempt to satisfy another longing, one for her remote, depressed mother. She chases a parental gaze which, when it comes, comes too late. Harrison and her father are both compelled to pin down the rapturous gaze of the elusive mother, and their relationship misguidedly serves this end. Her father,

> holding himself so still and staring at me, has somehow begun to *see* me into being. His look gives me to myself, his gaze reflects the life my mother's wilfully shut eyes denied. Looking at him looking at me, I cannot help but fall painfully, precipitously in love. And my loving him is inseparable from a piercing sense of loss.

Harrison is chasing the lost object, the object she never had—a warm, parental gaze that brings her into being. And together she and her father are chasing something they can never recapture: unity, merging, bliss.

*

It's no coincidence that Harrison makes use of fairytale tropes throughout *The Kiss*. Fairytales have often depicted the family as a site of violence—stepmothers poison stepdaughters, children are abandoned or eaten, rapacious fathers violate daughters. Harrison refers, for example, to Saint Dympna, a seventh-century Irish princess who escapes her pagan father's incestuous demands, fleeing with her confessor Gerbernus to Belgium. In Ghent, disguised as minstrels, the pair travel deep into the forest, build a hut out of branches, and live as hermits—not unlike Tom and her father in *Leave No Trace*, fleeing the ripple-effects of war.

Elizabeth Marshall has suggested that the rageful, disgusted responses of critics to Harrison's book echo the historical erasure of the incestuous father in Anglo-American fairytale collections, which themselves derive from the nineteenth-century collections of Charles Perrault and the Brothers Grimm. She cites Marian Cox's study of the 300-plus variants of the Cinderella story, in which Cox found that, in their earlier forms, an incestuous father appears almost as often as an evil stepmother. In the Cinderella story with which we are most familiar, the heroine is mistreated by a stepmother, while in its sibling story Catskin, a runaway daughter is pursued by an incestuous father; and in Cap O'Rushes—the story in which *King Lear* has its roots—a father demands a pledge of filial love. Heroines in the original stories Cox studied are as likely to leave the home because of a father's incestuous desire as her stepmother's tyranny. Yet incestuous fathers were effaced in collections such as the Brothers Grimm's *Children's and Household Tales*; for the one story in this collection that depicts a father's persecution of a daughter, there are twelve that recount a girl's travails at the hands of a stepmother.

For Marshall, *The Kiss* was incendiary to reviewers precisely because it disrupts the convention that an incest story requires a little girl rather than an adult grown woman as protagonist. Harrison, that is, shines the light back on to the abusive father—she returns his gaze. Nonetheless, Michael Kenny in *The Boston Globe* claimed that the book recounts an affair, not a case of sexual abuse, since Harrison was in her twenties, and the *Washington Post*, describing Harrison as seductive, 'not unwilling', states that *The Kiss* is 'a shameful book'. These critics silence Harrison's tale of the lustful father, just as history has edited out the rapacious patriarch in fairytales.

The traumatic effects of the incest, however, are clear. When Harrison's father rapes her, she writes that 'at that point I fall completely asleep... In years to come, I won't be able to remember even one instance of our lying together.' Throughout the book, the deadening sense of flight from her own self, her own life, could not be stronger. She remains with her father not out of a straightforward sexual desire for him, but out of a need to retain the affective ties between them. Or perhaps these two can amount to the same thing? By refusing to reduce incest to merely a physical act imposed on a little girl by an adult male, Harrison reveals the necessity of the stable yet flexible, reality-dosed mirroring that Winnicott talks about; the gaze that enables a child to individuate, and experience a sense of self. She reveals the curtailing of the self that arises from the lack of good-enough parenting—parenting that Winnicott saw as both utterly ordinary and immeasurably skilled. Without it, enchanted in all the dark ways enchantment can take place, Harrison is compelled to be seen at any exorbitant, self-thwarting price.

*

The idea of a desire, even an unconscious one, to sleep with the parent is easy enough either to ridicule, or to pass by with a horrified shudder. But the painful longing for an elusive parent—the desire to restore something that never existed, to redeem an absence—is conveyed in more ordinary ways by Susan Bordo in *The Male Body*. When, in her forties, she noticed her own proneness to dry skin, and in exactly the same places as her father's proneness, 'it came as a shock of startlingly precise, irrefutable linkage between him and me.' The 'shared malady, our dry skin, felt like intimacy.'

Bordo's father is a tyrannical brute not unlike Sylvie's in *Ghost Wall*; 'he owned our collective space absolutely—unconsciously, yet absolutely.' She describes her mother springing into action when her husband returns home, just as Moss depicts Sylvie's mother in *Ghost Wall* when Bill returns: 'Mum sat up as if someone had yanked her strings, and then lumbered to her feet.' Bordo's father's domination is similarly terrifying. But when he is dying, and Bordo is shocked by his frail state,

> what I was not prepared for was the deep comfort—perhaps it could even be called pleasure—that I got from simply being alone with him, close to his body, from holding his hand or touching his shoulder as long as I wanted to, from looking at him with such an unobstructed intimacy of gaze, from lingering with him and over him.

In a semi-wakeful, restful state, he accepts physical closeness and affection in a way he had never previously done. Her violent, bullish father is transformed into an infant, dependent on her for tenderness and care. He tells Bordo he is cold, and asks her to cover him.

When I did, he thanked me with the grace of a courtier, in the affectionate male lingo of his Runyonesque Brooklyn: 'Thank you, doll. Thank you, doll.' As wretched as he looked, I feasted on the sight of him as if he were my infant boy, and it was very hard to leave his side.

This is Bordo's longing—a longing unnervingly close to erotic love—for the mutual gaze of early life, a restitution of a withheld mirroring; a longing for the bodies from which we are made, the longing for a blissful union before we individuated, before we had to reckon with our hostility and hatred and leave the parental body.

*

In *The Girlfriend Experience*, Lodge Kerrigan and Amy Seimetz's 2016 television series, Riley

Keough plays Christine Read, a law student who also works as a high-end escort. The series is shot in a suffocatingly affectless tone, suffused with greyish greens and greenish greys, and surrounded with a constant low hum—the hum of office buildings and modern apartments, of air-conditioning or fridges subtly whirring. Much of the action is set in bland, minimalist offices—the law firm where Christine interns—or bland, anonymous apartments where she lives or visits clients.

Christine is hard-working and ambitious; Keough is impressively impassive and opaque. The series leaves open or unanswered, perhaps even unasked, the familiar and vexed questions of whether she enjoys her job, or is doing it autonomously, or experiencing any empowerment, or faking pleasure. The men— often middle-aged, dumpy, rich—say to her, 'I'd love to spend more time with you, I'd love to find a way to see you more'. She says, 'I would love that.' She is deadpan, but perhaps also she means it too. She is not gushing, she is not fake; but perhaps she is not quite for real either. The question isn't posed. Authenticity is not pivotal, and nor are causal narratives.

The men Christine has as clients are many things: successful, impulsive, frail, anxious, vulnerable, angry, controlling, distant. Many of them enjoy having an audience in Christine; sharing their problems, be they professional or personal. They enjoy having her undivided attention; an uncompromised feminine devotion. A devotion akin, perhaps to that of their mother, her gaze reflecting them back to themselves as infants; and akin, also, to their real or fantasised experiences of their daughters—Steve Martin's little girl, on a father's lap, leaning on his chest, listening, rapt, utterly absorbed in his presence. Perhaps what some men are getting from Christine is the feeling of being listened to, of being listened to in the way that a child, dependent on the mirroring of infancy and early childhood, listens to a parent. Christine's gaze is always steady; she is unflinching; she has an open, projective stare onto which illusions and desires can be projected. Perhaps she recalls, for the men, the devoted, enraptured attention of a child, a child in turn needing the gaze of the parent in order to assemble herself as real.

*

It's hard to reckon with where you come from. It's hard to disentangle the ranting, raving brutes from the modern, 'civilized' fathers; it's hard to figure out where to place your allegiance. In *Three Guineas,* Woolf describes an imagined procession of the sons of educated men, in all their garb and finery, and she writes, 'We have to ask ourselves, here and now, do we wish to join that procession, or don't we? On what terms shall we join that procession? Above all, where is it leading us, the procession of educated men?' The dilemma haunting her essay is this: how to 'join the professions and yet remain uncontaminated by them'.

One of the pressing tasks that our unsteady, unfolding #MeToo times ask of us is not just to confront our own status as victims of male dominance, but to reckon, too, with our own desires for retribution, revenge, and punishment; with our own fantasies of truth-telling and aggression. It's hard to examine your own family and its living presence within you, its presence with all its virtues and all its flaws. One thing I'm sure of, though: to reckon with our aggression and our hostility—to pursue a ruthless relation— to our roots is to be on the side of health. Concern for the object, compliance with it, are not the sign of love.

*

One of the patients in Alice Miller's book, *The Drama of Being a Child*, a book much influenced by Winnicott, describes the false self that Winnicott theorises in this way:

> I live in a glass house into which
> my mother could look at any time.
> In a glass house, you cannot conceal
> anything without giving yourself
> away, except by hiding it under the
> ground. And then you cannot see it
> yourself, either.

If the mother forces the infant to see her, she drives the infant's self into hiding. A child with a mother who is intrusively demanding—an unresponsive mother, or a mother whose face is frozen by a depressed mood—is forced to perceive the mother, and to read her mood at the cost of its own feelings being recognised. This need to 'look after mother's mood' is an early form of compliance, which will distract the child from its own development.

The point is not that there is a fully developed, 'true self' consciously lying in wait behind the false self; it is that the child does not know what, or even that, it is hiding. The child is both constantly visible, yet strangely absent. It is in hiding, and yet too much in the bright, coercive glare of the parent's own needs. It is in a glass house; all too seen, yet unable to see itself.

For Winnicott, deeply shaped by the ideas of Melanie Klein, aggression was crucial to development. The mother, in response to the infant's destructive impulses, must not allow herself to be destroyed, and she must not retaliate. If she can survive the full blast of the subject's destructiveness, then and only then can the subject, the baby, conceive of her, the object, as beyond its power and therefore fully real. The object only becomes real to the infant by being hated. As Alison Bechdel puts it in *Are You My Mother?*, the child needs an object it can destroy, and who will survive that destruction. If the object survives the destruction, the subject—the child—can see both itself and the object as separate. If the object doesn't survive, it will remain internal, a projection of the subject's self; and nothing will seem real.

Toni Erdmann, Maren Ade's 2016 film, depicts the echoes of this dynamic in adult life. It opens with a young woman, Ines, visiting her family at home in Germany. Ines has a corporate job in Bucharest; she is successful—busy, stressed, beleaguered. On the visit, she is abrupt and evasive, faking phone calls to avoid sitting at dinner, and seems desperate to get back to her own life— one which, we soon discover, is flat, lonely, and constrained.

Ines works for an oil firm, as a consultant specialising in corporate outsourcing, against the backdrop of a fast-changing, globalising Romania—'we have the biggest mall in Europe', someone says, 'and no one has the money to buy anything'. Her work life is dominated by men; colleagues discuss whether to 'bring my wife over'; Ines gets palmed off by an important visiting associate to go shopping with his wife.

Shortly after Ines' trip home, her father makes a surprise visit to Bucharest, where he embarks on a series of disorienting, uncomfortable pranks, all involving the wearing of grotesque false teeth and an unruly wig. This is Toni Erdmann, an alter ego of sorts. Ines goes along with the pranks, mostly out of stunned awkwardness, and accepts him reluctantly as a visitor. He tries to be kind and show care, but she is prickly and aggressive. When he asks if she is happy at work, she cruelly fires the question back at him. 'What do *you* find worth living for?' she asks.

He is out of his depth, while she is locked in to her unhappiness. Eventually, he decides to leave; they say goodbye affectionately. The first time we see her smile a real smile is when she waves goodbye to him from her balcony. And then she weeps. It turns out, though, that he has not left; he accosts her later, in his bizarre get-up as Toni Erdmann—a life coach—at a bar where she is with friends. In the following days, he turns up at her work, too. At no point does she disclose his identity, and they develop an odd, bristling companionship.

Ines decides to organise a party, and the preparation is stressful; everything is work, there is no pleasure. On a seeming whim, she opens the door to her friend and assistant naked. When her boss arrives, she tells him it's a naked party. He leaves, only to return later, duly undressed; others arrive; there is awkward conversation. Someone gives her a present, and she is tearful. What is happening? We sense her unravelling, unable to shore herself up against her own sadness.

And then an arresting figure appears, in a strange, furry costume entirely covering the wearer's body and face. It shimmers, its long hair fluttering, rippling disconcertingly. Its head is large, oblong, tall, and unwieldy; the creature moves lumberingly, unsteadily, as if in slow, awkward motion. The guests are frozen in alarm, confusion; ordinary life halts. The creature moves about, surrounded by a stunned silence, and then leaves, a vision from another world. Ines frantically gets dressed and follows it out of the building, down the street, into a park. She knows, just as we do, that this is her father. In the park, she catches up with him— he has been lurching slowly, strangely, watched by curious observers—and says, 'Papa', and they embrace. Everything thaws, everything unravels.

Throughout, Ines' father has enacted a series of masks and pretences in order to try to breach the gap between himself and his daughter. And father and daughter have played; the pretence and absurdity they've been through, with its risks and discomforts, has enabled her feelings to move. Reality has intruded, in the form of play. It is in his final masked form—this haunting, disconcerting, not quite human form—that the projections, misunderstandings, and delusions can fall away, and daughter and father can meet in reality.

In *Are You My Mother?*, Alison Bechdel writes that 'I wish Winnicott were my mother.' It's a painful moment of recognition, a reckoning with failures of parenting in her life. She describes Winnicott's pragmatic, ordinary, humane methods of conducting therapy with children. She draws him down on the floor with a little girl, his legs up in the air. 'Winnicott', she says, 'played, too.'

But it's hard to play when you are scared—it's hard to play with someone you fear. And it's hard to love if you cannot express hate; if all you can feel in the gaze of the parent is anxiety about your love, or a request for it. Love cannot be demanded, as King Lear does of Cordelia. And it has to incorporate hostility.

Creating the capacity for love is the hardest thing a parent has to do, and it is hard for parents to do it if they need love from the child in order to feel themselves to be real.

If you're the kind of person who needs love, mused an interviewer on 'Unconditional Love', a *This American Life* episode about attachment, chances are you are not the kind of person who has the wherewithal to create it. '*Nothing, my Lord*', said Cordelia to her father when he demanded a display of her love. *I cannot heave my heart into my mouth.*

It is perhaps crucial that when Ines' father takes on his uncanny form, in his otherworldly costume, she cannot see his face; he has no face to see. She is free of his anxiety to make her happy, or his unhappiness at her misery. She can, while he is in masked form, experience him as real. The opposite of play, writes Adam Phillips, glossing Winnicott, is not work, but coercion. When Ines feels coerced into being happy—into being something for her father—she cannot play. But when he dissembles himself, she is uncoerced; she is free to play, free to hate, and therefore free to love; free to inhabit her feelings, and to see her father—the object she wanted to destroy—survive her attempts at destruction. Only then can she see him as real, and only then can she exist as herself.

*

Gornick, in *Fierce Attachments*, wrote about feeling nauseatingly porous with her mother. She wrote too about feeling un-seen by her, and conveys something familiar by now: a child acutely attuned to the parent's ever-changing, unpredictable moods.

> Nor does she know she's wiping me out. She doesn't know I take her anxiety personally, feel annihilated by her depression. How can she know this? She doesn't even know I'm there.

Not to be seen by the mother is not to exist, and being seen, thought Winnicott, is the condition for creative looking. It's no accident that Gornick writes so powerfully about annihilation and merging, and also expresses so powerfully the psychological elation of writing itself. In her book on non-fiction, *The Situation and the Story*, she describes how she felt on discovering the narrator for *Fierce Attachments*, saying that she experienced

> an absorption that in time went unequaled. I longed each day to meet up again with her, this other one telling the story that I alone—in my everyday person—would not have been able to tell. I could hardly believe my luck in having found her (that's what it felt like, luck). It was not only that I admired her style, her generosity, her detachment—such a respite from the me that was me!—she had become the instrument of my illumination.

The book makes the case for finding and

honing a persona—one who is 'me and not-me'—as the necessary condition for writing good first-person material, for being able to make a story out of a mere situation. It is no coincidence that a writer who conveys with such precision the experience of having a depressed parent can also convey the somewhat alienated, uncanny, ghostly writing self that lies both inside and beside the writer; the excitingly other person through whom she is able to write. It is also no coincidence that this persona Gornick describes, a persona characterised by generosity and detachment, could also function as a description of Winnicott's good-enough mother. The Gornick that is 'me and not me'—'such a respite from the me that was not me!'—and who can write her books, is both warm and detached; generous, but ruthless; the exact, delicate, difficult combination of parenting qualities that Winnicott so painstakingly described. Gornick, in writing, has created a parent who sees Gornick the child and reflects her back to herself, and a parent who is simultaneously capable of withstanding Gornick's aggression. She has created, in others, her own good-enough mother.

*

For Freud, aggression was a reaction to reality, a frustration with the world's failure to instantly satisfy our needs and desires. Winnicott saw things differently, turning this structure on its head; we rarely hear, he wrote, of the 'relief and satisfaction' that reality affords. The child, in order to develop a sense of self that is not a prop for a parent, has to be allowed to feel aggression and hatred for that parent, rather than living in fear of, and inventively avoiding, provoking the parent's hostility. It's not, then, that reality makes us feel aggression. It's that aggression makes us feel real.

Writing, especially if it touches on difficult

topics, is often cast as therapeutic—not least by writers themselves, as writing does often turn out to be therapeutic. But when someone asks me if writing is therapeutic, I generally feel it's the wrong question. The more accurate formulation, for me, is that writing is how I experience my experience. Until writing, in mere living, everything is out of focus; in mere living, I comply with demands. Trained to liveliness, I react to stimuli. I am only, as Winnicott puts it, 'playing for time.'

Writing is different. There, I turn my back on others, and turn my back on their needs; I cannot see their anxious, demanding gazes. Writing is where I leave my state of suspended animation, and start on my own life. It is where I refuse the expectation of compliance, and where I can feel my aggression. It's where I go to be deeply, and freely alone; to create myself, and experience myself as real. Writing is the medium sufficiently resilient to withstand the full blast of it all. Through writing, I create a parent, an other, whose face remains impassive, who doesn't demand my false self. In writing, I create the object—the reader—the father—I can destroy, and who will survive that destruction.

Works Cited

Alison Bechdel, *Are You My Mother? A Comic Drama* (Jonathan Cape, 2012)

Alison Bechdel, *Fun Home: A Family Tragicomic* (Jonathan Cape, 2006)

Jessica Benjamin, *The Bonds of Love: Psychoanalysis, Feminism, and the Problem of Domination* (Pantheon Books, 1988)

Susan Bordo, *The Male Body: A New Look at Men in Public and in Private* (Farrar, Straus, & Giroux, 2001)

Marian Cox, *Cinderella: Three Hundred and Forty-Five Variants of Cinderella, Catskin, and Cap O'Rushes* (Andrew Lang, 1893).

Sigmund Freud, *The Interpretation of Dreams* (Allen, 1954) (first published 1899)

Vivian Gornick, *Fierce Attachments: A Memoir* (Farrar, Straus, & Giroux, 1987) (first published in the UK by Daunt Books in 2015)

Vivian Gornick, *The Situation and the Story: The Art of Personal Narrative* (Farrar, Straus, & Giroux, 2001)

Kathryn Harrison, *The Kiss* (Fourth Estate, 1997)

bell hooks, 'Revolutionary Parenting', in *Feminist Theory: From Margin to Center* (Boston: South End Press, 1984)

Michael Kenney, 'The Naked Truth', *Boston Globe*, 8 April 1997

Jacques Lacan, *Ecrits: A Selection* (Tavistock, 1980)

Hermione Lee, *Virginia Woolf* (Vintage, 1997)

Sophie Mackintosh, *The Water Cure* (Hamish Hamilton, 2018)

Elizabeth Marshall, 'The Daughter's Disenchantment: Incest as Pedagogy in Fairy Tales and Kathryn Harrison's *The Kiss*', *College English*, 66(4), March 2004, pp 403-426.

Alice Miller, 'How We Became Psychotherapists', in *The Drama of Being a Child* (Virago, 2014)(first published 1979), translated by Ruth Ward.

Sarah Moss, *Ghost Wall* (Farrar, Straus, & Giroux, 2018)

Jenny Offil, *Dept. of Speculation* (Knopf, 2014)

Sharon Olds, *The Unswept Room* (Jonathan Cape, 2003)

Adam Phillips, *Winnicott* (Penguin, 2007) (first

published in 1988)

William Shakespeare, *King Lear*, ed. R.A. Foakes (Arden, 1997)

Peter Sheridan and Caroline Graham, '"Perhaps it'd be easier if I was dead": Heartbroken Thomas Markle Says His Daughter is Ignoring Him', *Daily Mail*, 28 July 2018

Valerie Solanas, *SCUM Manifesto* (Verso, 2015, originally published Olympia Press 1971)

Leslie Stephen, letters to Charles Norton, 23 Aug 1896, 10 Jan 1897, cited in Hermione Lee, *Virginia Woolf*

Jia Tolentino, 'One Year of #MeToo: What Women's Speech is Still Not Allowed To Do', *New Yorker*, October 10, 2018

James Walcott, 'The 20-year-old Who Dated Her Dad—and then Wrote A Book About It', *The New*

Republic, 31 March 1997

Donald Winnicott, 'The Manic Defence', 1935, in *Collected Papers: Through Paediatrics to Psycho-analysis* (Tavistock, 1958)

Donald Winnicott, 'Home Again', 1945, in *Deprivation and Delinquency* (London: Tavistock, 1984)

Donald Winnicott, 'Reparation in Respect of Mother's Organized Defence Against Depression', 1948, in *Collected Papers: Through Paediatrics to Psycho-analysis* (Tavistock, 1958)

Donald Winnicott, 'Group Influences and the Maladjusted Child', 1955, in *The Family and Individual Development* (Tavistock, 1964)

Donald Winnicott, 'Mirror-Role of Mother and Family in Child Development', 1967, in *Therapeutic Consultations in Child Psychiatry* (The Hogarth Press and the Institute of Psycho-analysis 1971)

Donald Winnicott, 'The Use of an Object and Relating Through Identifications', 1969, in *Playing and Reality* (Tavistock, 1971)

Virginia Woolf, *Three Guineas*, Penguin (1977) (first published by The Hogarth Press, 1938)

Virginia Woolf, 'Reminiscences', *Moments of Being* (ed. Jeanne Schulkind, Sussex University Press, 1976, revised 1985)

Virginia Woolf, 'Memoir', 18 July 1939, A5C, Monk's House Papers, University of Sussex Library Manuscript Collections

Jonathan Yardley, 'Daddy's Girl Cashes In: Kathryn Harrison Writes a Shameful Memoir of Incest', *Washington Post*, 5 March 1997.

Films
Ginger and Rosa, written and directed by Sally

Potter, 2012

Leave No Trace, directed by Debra Granik, 2018 (screenplay by Debra Granik and Anne Rosellini, based on *My Abandonment* by Peter Rock)

The Father of the Bride, directed by Charles Shyer, 1991 (screenplay by Charles Shyer, Nancy Meyers, Frances Goodrich, Albert Hackett)

Meet the Parents, directed by Jay Roach, 2001, screenplay written by Jim Herzfeld and John Hamburg

Toni Erdmann, written and directed by Maren Ade, 2016

Leaving Neverland, directed by Dan Reed, 2019

Other media

'Unconditional Love, *This American Life*, episode 317, September 15, 2006: Act One: Love is a

Battlefield, Alix Spiegel

Garth Greenwell, *Literary Salon podcast*, March 2016

Ivanka Trump, interview on the Late Show with David Letterman, 2007 (https://www.youtube.com/watch?v=cWNgMiquWfo, last accessed 28 April 2019)

Donald Trump, *The View*, 2006 (https://www.youtube.com/watch?v=DP7yf8-Lk8o, last access 28 April 2019)

Donald Trump, *Howard Stern Show*, 2003 (https://www.youtube.com/watch?v=8EPEkk6qWkg, last accessed 28 April 2019)

The Girlfriend Experience, written and directed by Lodge Kerrigan and Amy Seimetz, 2016

Anthea Hamilton's *The Squash*, Tate Britain, March-October 2018.

Thanks

My thanks to Sam Fisher and Peninsula Press for suggesting I write for the press—and to Sam, Jake Franklin, and Will Rees for their thoughtful and insightful editing. Thank you to Cassie Robinson and the late Roanne Dods for a residency at Cove Park in 2014 in which I first explored some of these ideas, and to Charlotte Shane, who when commissioning me for *On Balance* (TigerBee Press) in 2016, also helped open a door on this material. Thank you to Georgina Evans and Isabelle McNeill for inviting me to the Tactics and Praxis seminar at Cambridge University in 2018, where I discussed some of these questions. Thank you to my colleagues and students at Birkbeck College, University of London. And the deepest thanks go to Allie Carr, Hannah Dawson, Alyssa Harad, Francesca Joseph, Sasha Mudd, Rebecca Tamás, Rachel Warrington, and to my family: Ros, David, and Mitzi Angel, and Matthew Sperling and Buddy.

Peninsula Press would like to thank Larry Coppersmith and Dominic Franklin for their continued support.

Other titles available in this series

Mixed-Race Superman by Will Harris
(ISBN: 9781999922306)

A personal essay on Barrack Obama, Keanu Reeves and mixed-race experience in our increasingly divided world.

At once personal and political, *Mixed-Race Superman* is a reflection on the lives of two very different supermen: Barack Obama and Keanu Reeves. In an era where a man endorsed by the Klu Klux Klan can sit in the White House, Will Harris argues that the mixed-race background of each gave them a shapelessness that was a form of resistance. Reeves, as Neo in *The Matrix*, portrayed the chosen one on the silver screen, while Obama, for a brief moment, took the shape of a superhero on the world stage.

Drawing on his own personal experience and examining the way that these two men have been embedded in our collective consciousness, Will Harris asks what they can teach us about race and heroism.

***Exposure* by Olivia Sudjic**
(ISBN: 9781999922337)

An essay on the anxiety epidemic, autofiction and
internet feminism.

After the release of *Sympathy*, her debut novel which
explores surveillance and identity in the internet age,
Olivia Sudjic found herself under the microscope.
Trapped in an anxious spiral of self-doubt, she became
alienated from herself and her work. Blaming her
own mental-health masked a wider problem that still
persists: the tendency for writing by women, whether
fiction or personal testimony, to be invalidated on the
grounds of sex.

Drawing on Sudjic's experience of anxiety - as well as
the work of Elena Ferrante, Maggie Nelson, Jenny Offill,
Rachel Cusk and others *Exposure* examines the damaging
assumptions that attend female artists, indeed any
woman who risks exposure, as well as the strategies by
which one might escape them.

Please visit peninsulapress.co.uk to order,
or for more information.